Happiness and savings

We all can be happy and have savings, we just have to know where to focus our attention and have a reason to save.

Omar El Bachiri was born on January 5, 1977 in Morocco, in a small town in the Nador province. At the age of two, he moved with his family to the Principality of Andorra. Today he continues living in the same country. He has a Clinical Psychology degree by the UNED. His greatest passion is traveling and he practices sport daily.

Omar El Bachiri

Happiness and Savings

A book translated into French with thousands of copies sold in several countries around the world.

The guide to know how to be happy with what you already have and learn to save.

You will get the habit to smile every day and save a portion of your incomes.

Written and edited by Omar El Bachiri

All rights reserved. It is strictly forbidden the partial or total reproduction of this work by any means or procedure, whether electronic or mechanical, without the prior written permission of the copyright holder, under the penalties established by law.

2015 Omar El Bachiri El Boudouhi Copyright ©,

Original title: Feliz y con Ahorros

ISBN: 978-99920-3-122-3

Legal deposit: AND-557-2016

First edition: December 2016

English translation: Genoveva Gutiérrez Ruiz

Index:

1. P.9 Acknowledgements.
2. P.10 Prologue.
3. P.15 Observations on the two forms of being rich.
4. P.17 Basic needs.
5. P.18 Life is changing.
6. P.19 Good or bad, depends on you.
7. P.20 Intelligent optimistic.
8. P.21 Get the better from worse.
9. P.22 Why you work?
10. P.23 Reason to argue.
11. P.24 Time and money.
12. P.26 Work´s importance.
13. P.27 The three brother´s case.
14. P.29 John´s problem.
15. P.31 Money and happiness relation.
16. P.34 Judge yourself by what you are capable of.
17. P.36 The artists.
18. P.36 Positive and proactive attitudes.
19. P.39 Thinking of preferring instead of should of.
20. P.40 It's not the situation nor the adversity fault.
21. P.40 The traffic light model.
22. P.43 Three steps to appreciate your job.
23. P.44 The importance of saving.
24. P.45 Simple habits to grow older then right way.
25. P.46 Save always the 20% of your incomes.
26. P.49 Financial intelligence.
27. P.51 Three habits to have money always.
28. P.51 The banks.

29. P.53 Credit card benefits.
30. P.54 Where and how the money is spent.
31. P.59 Don´t be ashamed of your economy.
32. P.60 Shopping.
33. P.61 Assets and liabilities.
34. P.62 Poor and rich mindset.
35. P.64 Save and invest are not the same.
36. P.66 The football player.
37. P.66 The Passerby and the Explorer.
38. P.67 Good and bad debts.
39. P.69 How to pay several debts at the same time.
40. P.72 Happiness.
41. P.74 Smiling.
42. P.75 Smile in front of the mirror.
43. P.76 Learning.
44. P.77 Assuming responsibilities.
45. P.79 Learning at school.
46. P.80 Don't get attached to material.
47. P.81 Fear of death.
48. P.82 The case of Oscar.
49. P.83 Living being yourself.
50. P.84 Achieving our goals.
51. P.89 Leisure.
52. P.91 Pretending.
53. P.93 Compilation of motivational phrases.

Acknowledgements: I want to express my grateful to my couple, Fanny, whom I explained a big part of the book's ideas for discussion and especially for helping me to express them in a clear and concise way. Since it would be impossible to list all them, I also want to thank my friends who directly or indirectly contributed to the result of this book.

In particular, **Tano** and **Bego**, for our many conversations on all topics covered in it and that motivated me to write it.

I also want to thank the **River Mall bookstore**, for their trust in my book and being the first to sell it nationwide. From there, my name started out in the media and everything was easier.

And finally, I want to thank the customers of **Lugo Bar**. Cradle of my theories about happiness, they are so optimistic and happy that I am inspired by the way they perceive and interpret life.

Prologue

The relationship between money and happiness is a subject that always intrigued me. I couldn't understand why rich people weren't able to be happy. Having money, cars, properties, travels, well, all the necessary to be happy.

I get them being sad every now and then. They are humans too. But unhappy? I couldn´t understand. As it is a subject that interests me a lot, I researched about it and I have drawn my own conclusions.

Has been a several years' research. Talking to people from around the world and from different social classes, from millionaires to homeless. Travelling through several continents, countries, cities and towns.

I´ll write those conclusions in this book and hope they are right for you. Once you read them, I hope you understand, as well as I did, and put your life in perspective, because perspective enables us to enjoy to the fullest.

I want to warn you, dear reader, that this book will be disappointed if you trust that you are going to find in it something really innovative.

I'm not trying to invent any theory or formula that makes you change your way of being. Nor will make you happy and saver overnight.

If you want to see this change, you'll have to get involved. I mention how to have savings, not how to be a millionaire.

I will explain the reasons of saving, how to save without giving up and how to be happy with what you already have.

Depends exclusively of you the change that you can make, what I can assure you, is that if you follow these guidelines that I put in the book, you will get it.

The book is aimed to everyone, but those who most benefit will get, are those that working all year, aren´t able to save anything once the year ends and those who complain endlessly about their economic and/or family situation.

I hope and wish with all my heart that reading **"Happiness and Savings"** help you live the life you want and feel really happy.

It develops in two different parts, with several independent chapters, but the theme of saving links them all. I consider it a very important topic if you want to enjoy the desired life.

Part one

Observations on economic wealth and well - being:

Once in a while there we have to be compared with others, to see how we are in our lives, either on an economic or sentimental level.

But it must be done in different types of social environments, not only in our environment.

It must be done with people who earn the same amount of money that we earn, people who earn more and less. Thus, we can see how they deal with life and draw conclusions regarding ourselves and the best way to do it... is traveling.

For several countries, cities and towns. If for whatever reason you cannot travel out of your country, nothing happens. Travels through your own country, go through different places and find out the standard of living of those sites.

How many hours people works per day and how much they earn monthly. How they spent their money, their way of seeing life and how they live it.

Because we can be rich economically but poor in wellness, what is all about, it is to be rich and happy. With a little will and effort both concepts can be joined.

Economic wealth:

It is calculated in time and not in absolute value as it is tended to think.

Quitting your work now, how many days you would be able to maintain the same way of life? one week, one month, years?

There are people who seem rich because they have many possessions, but if they stop working for just two weeks, they are ruined. They are people who have more expenses than income. However, there are others that could be fine for years without working. Later I delved into this subject.

Welfare:

To have welfare we need to know which ones are the basic needs and which are simply for pleasure, also necessary but not essential. Distinguish them is welfare.

To taste it, we must celebrate any event that makes us feel good and above all, that has supposed an effort.

It may be, pass an exam, have reduced the electricity bill, phone bill, lose weight, etc.

Never stop enjoying an achievement by an adverse situation. If you do, you'll focus on the negative and the positive side will stop. It makes no sense to get your goals in life if when you are about to taste them, focus your attention on the negative around you.

You made an effort and your reward is to enjoy it and taste it.

Rejoice in the pleasure of having achieved your goals.

Never underestimate your accomplishments.

The basic needs for survival are two: Nutrition (food and drink) and shelter.

Having this cover, you will search for others, such as: security, love, social and self-realization.

We all seek to cover these basic needs. In prehistoric times, the caveman was hunting for food and looking for a cave to have refuge and feel secure. From there, seek to relate to more people, find a mate to procreate and raise a family. Curiously, the country with the highest level of happiness in the world is Bhutan and not Germany or the United States, as you might think.

Is a country located in South Asia, at the foot of the eastern end of the Himalayas, considered a third world country. While conventional economic models use the Gross Domestic Product (GDP) to see economic growth as the main objective, the government this country uses the concept of (GNH) Gross National Happiness. It is based on the premise that true development of human society is on the complementarity and mutual reinforcement of material and spiritual development.

Its aim is to enhance human well-being from the guarantee of certain rights and social parameters and not to promote the pursuit of having materials. They are aware that material is necessary to lead a more comfortable life, but they are not obsessed in acquiring it.

Life is changing, is in constant motion:

We must never forget that the world is changing, although the situation seems still in fact it is not.A simple change in someone´s life of your environment can disrupt your whole world.

So, too good or too bad your life is going, is temporary. If it's good, learn and enjoy it and if it is bad, learn and be patient. For many problems you may have, you do not know if certain day, the person you have a problem has awake in a good mood for whatever reason and solve the problem with you. Moreover, what is a problem today, tomorrow perhaps it is no longer and becomes a story.

A simple change in your life can disrupt your whole environment.

Good or bad, it depends on how you see it. It may be a problem or not:

There was a guy at the airport waiting for boarding time to board the plane and go on vacation. A few minutes before boarding he was notified that his flight was canceled to the next day.

- The man calls by phone to his parents to inform them and they tell him:
- What a bad luck, to which the boy replied: Bad or good, who knows?
- The next day the airline decides to compensate, running with all the expenses he may have during his vacation to what his parents say:
- What a good luck and the boy answer again: Good or bad, who knows?
- After arriving at the hotel and rest, he had a scheduled tour, but decides not to go because as the airline will pay all costs the he decides to take a better one.

The tour bus had an accident and all were injured and had to be admitted into a hospital. Again the parents said, good luck that you changed your mind... and so on...

Luck depends on the point of view, it can be good or bad.

Always we have to be thankful just to be alive, breathing and living in the so-called first world. This will lead us to be optimistic. But smart optimistic.

Smart Optimistic:

I mean, not just thinking, I will be optimistic and everything will go well for me. The smart optimism is linked to proactivity.

Is not just think that everything is fine although everything is bad, it is not to deny reality. It is to accept it as it is, but thinking that you can change it, that with a little effort you can change the situation.

It's not about to sit still until life pass to find this good chance. You have to make things happen and go get them. That good chance we have to create it, focus on the wonderful things that life offers us and squeeze the maximum.

Being grateful, we will complain in perspective, when we see an unfair situation and want to improve it. If you won't act, do not complain. Isn't useful. If the other party doesn't see a move won't feel threatened and will not change.

> **Complain and not act creates bad atmosphere in the environment.**

Benefit yourself from bad times:

Bad times also have their reason to be. When you are going through a bad time, people are there for us. They pamper and care for us to make us feel better and also we do things that we´ll never do in another state. Whereupon, you can learn new forms of behavior and experiences. You also have to taste the sadness but rejoice in it.

When you are sad: you see gloomy movies, read books of love, listen slow music. Would you do it if you were not sad? You would see action movies, comic books and would read adventure books.

Therefore, is good and even healthy to have negative emotions, we must be able to distinguish it to recognize them. Never hold back, let them emerge in the right measure. They're to warn us that something is wrong. When we go through a bad situation, we feel sad and down, it's normal, we are human.

The issue here is to stop and think:

What can be done to overcome this situation?
What for this is happened? and look for the good side, which is the one that will benefit us.

Every situation has a negative part and another positive, let´s focus on the positive one.

Before continuing I invite you to answer the following questions:

- Why do you work?
- What will you do with the money you earn? If you just want to cover your basic needs, you will not need much.
- Why do you want to earn more money through working harder, exchange time for money?

Time is the only thing that is not recovered once lost, either given away or sold. So that´s why we are paying for exchange it, is an exchange of favors. I do something for you and you give me money. Appreciate who gives you its time, is giving you the most valuable of its life.

As for the money, it is like energy, is not destroyed, but transformed. It is passed from hand to hand. Sometimes it becomes something material such as a car, a house, more money and sometimes something subjective as welfare. This transformation is really important because money is a means to cover our basic needs.

As these needs, they are followed closely by one that is truly important, love. Love understood not only as love couple, but as having someone with whom to share moments, interact and express what we feel anytime without fear of being judged by our ideas and thoughts. If you do not have this last need cover, you can live as well, but without having a pleasant life.

> To fully enjoy we must share.

The two reasons for discussion:

In a couple or family there are only two reasons to discuss, lack of money and/or lack of love. As one of this two walks through the door, the other goes out through the window.

With money, you can go on vacation, go out to dinner, buy gifts to family and reach a pleasant level of living. With love, you can enjoy pleasant conversations, enjoy the company of your children, family and friends. When you're going through a bad time, you have where to lean morally.

If one of these is missing, the balance is broken.

It must be a harmony between money and love, work enough to have the necessary. Because although money is not the most important thing in the world, it is directly related to what it is, basic needs and pleasure.

With basic we are already happy but if we can get the pleasure, we'll have an even more pleasant life.

Work enough to have the necessary.

As I mentioned earlier, time is the most valuable thing that we have as humans:

A terminally ill person will give anything to have more time. If you are not convinced of what I say, try to go to the hospital to visit people who are in this phase and pass time with them.

Listen to what they will say, most believe that time is very valuable. Who better than them to value time?
In this life, you only regret what you didn't do, having missed so many opportunities to have done what you really liked.

Time and money:

Ana is a woman of 35, is an economist and works for a renowned firm of Internet sales, is happily married and has two children.

She works every day, including weekends. Its goal is to get one million of euros to have the desired life and to spend more time with her family. When her husband, children or friends suggest to go to the movies or out for a drink, she always answers them *not now*, she has to get that million to then spend time with them.

Ana, now 55 years old, has achieved her cherished million of euros, but her friends no longer calls, her husband has left her and their children are now independent.

One day they someone rings the bell of her home and she opens the door, in front there was a dressed in black and smiling being.

- Hey, it says. I am death and come to get you, now is your time.
- Surprised replied, no. You can't take me with you. Now I have a million euros and I can do whatever I want.
- Let's make a deal she says, I'll give you ten thousand euros if you give me two more years of life.
- No, replied death.
- Well, a hundred thousand euros, Ana proposes.
- Death doesn't change.
- Half a million for a month of life.
- Being negative the answer of death.
- Desperately she proposes to give one million euros for a few seconds of life, to say goodbye to their loved ones, again death responds no.
- Your time has come and you come with me, sorry.

Lesson of the story: Neither one million of euros can buy even a second of time. Life is what happens while we make plans.

If you do not know for how long you're going to be alive, act and enjoy the pleasures that life offers.

| **Life is a gift, don't waste it.** |

The importance of work:

As for the person, individually, this is the third reason for discussion.

If one of the three fails, the person is uncomfortable.

When a job is accepted, you must answer these three questions:

I accept it:

1. Because the money I'll earn?
2. Because the free time I'll get?
3. Because I like it?

As soon as we know the right answer, we will know how to focus our attitude toward it.

If accepted because salary, chances are that eventually we feel frustrated, even more if they reduce it because reasons not in our hands. So you have to think about it as a source of income that allows us to have the desired life once the workday finish.

If accepted by the free time left, it's the same as in the previous situation. We will focus it to enjoy once we finish work.

But unlike the previous case, if it does not depend on the income, you enjoy more, because although we reduce the salary, we will be happy because our goal is leisure time.

If accepted because we like it, we have won the lottery.

In this case, there will be no problem to go to work. Even if our salary is reduced, as long as we cover basic needs and left something for leisure, we will fell complete.

Everything depends on the reason, what we're looking for our lives at this moment.

That's why we should not close doors to other jobs, other forms of income, since each stage of life we look for something different. The more you learn from each job and situation better. You never know if there will be a source of income from it in the future.

The three brothers case:

Charles, James and Carla.

All three work in the same aluminum factory. Charles is the older, he is 39, James the middle one, has 37 and the youngest Carla has 35 years.

They all have the same time in the factory, 8 years. Charles got it because the salary, James, for free time and Carla because she liked as it made an FP in managing aluminum and she felt realized.

For reasons out of their hands, especially crisis, their salary is reduced by 20%.

Charles, his motive is money, has been sick of his work for long and in top of that they lower his salary, he does not like his job at all. Until now he was holding, but because of a debt, the income that he receive is no longer enough because it has little money once paid the debts, he is frustrated. He is stuck in a job that do not satisfies him, neither personally nor financially.

James, his motive is free time, he doesn't really like his job. But as has many days off and flexible schedules, he can travel, play sports and study from distance. This is his main motivation to go there. Even they lowered its salary, it is enough to have the desired life.

Carla, her motive is that she likes it, she is the luckiest. She works on what she really like, she has turn her work into a hobby.

Even when they had lowered the salary she feels realized and is confident that when the situation improves, it will go up again and if not, when she ascends and charge more. Because she like its job, she works hard and learn every day, not only does the minimum to spend 8 hours. She wants to become the director of the factory.

Of the three cases, the best situation would be to have a little of each. Good pay, free time and that we like it. Hence the above three questions.

Make from your work a passion and not a necessity.

John´s problem, he not relativizes life:

John could be any of you who are reading the book.
Although I've use a masculine name that no one misleads, could also be a woman called Mary.

John: I have a problem and I've been thinking about it for several days.

It all started a few weeks ago when I met Peter, my childhood friend. It was 10 years since we met, since I went to Switzerland to study.

We started talking about life, how we were and what we have done over the years and then I doubt about something.

While we were talking, he didn't stop smiling, he told me how good life is going. He works in the neighborhood cardboard factory, he is not that excited about it, but as the shop where he used to work closed… he only found this place.They do not pay much but it is enough to pay debts to the bank as he borrowed money to buy furniture for the floor where he was living, a car, pay for college and still has a bit to go for a drink with friends or to the movies with his girlfriend.

He is studying law at university at night and he had to return to live with their parents because he has not enough to pay the rent. He feels very happy with the life he leads and considered it successful, because he had always wanted to study law and finally he is doing it.

Now I´ll explain my problem:

I'm 28 years and 3 years ago, finished my medical studies. I have 2 years working as an assistant in my father's clinic to gain experience because I want to study a master's degree in plastic surgery. I have a salary of 2,000 euros a month, for my expenses. I have a new car, I own an apartment and a girlfriend. I also consider myself as successful.

Lately I work 12 hours a day and barely have time to be with my girlfriend and friends. But I should do it if I want to get that master and make my father proud of me.

Eventually he will let me run the hospital, he wants to retire. That's my dream, to direct the hospital. Having all this I should feel good but it's quite the opposite, I feel lonely, sad, anxious, empty. When I buy something, soon after it no longer satisfied me and I must buy something else. I do not understand how Peter having less than I, is so happy and feel successful?

Easy John, I'll show you the relationship between money and happiness so you can understand why your friend Peter is happy and you not.

The relationship between money and happiness:

It is a curious fact, because once reached certain level of life where make it until the month ends is no longer a problem and our real needs are cover, more money does not make us happier.

It allows us to live more comfort and more amenities, but that's it. However, the quantity and quality of interpersonal relationships is a factor that is associated with a higher level of happiness or what is the same, a greater psychological wellbeing.
As I mentioned above, these requirements are:

1- Having to eat (food and water).
2- Having a shelter.

Another very important once covered these two, is to have access to healthcare.

The human being you just want to eat and drink, have somewhere to rest, when sick, to heal. Once you have these cover will go for other needs, such as love, friendship, a better job, improve quality of life, etc...

I summarize it in a simple way for you to understand:

When you're hungry and/or thirsty and you cannot be satisfied, don´t you get in a bad mood? You just look to satisfied that need and you don´t feel comfortable, right? and when you have eaten and/or drunk, you say to yourself: Oh, I feel well!

When it's cold, it's raining, snowing or is very hot, don´t you want to be somewhere quiet and safe to take shelter, waiting for better weather?

Having a place to rest after a working day where you have your privacy?

When you get a hand injured, a leg... headache, toothache, stomach, etc. Would you like going to the doctor and be able to pay for treatment, right?

What if you could not pay for it? Surely you lose the hand or leg or you would die for an oral infection.
Having these needs cover you are the happiest person on the planet.

Once you have them covered you can go for your other needs. But do not forget that the essential thing to be happy, you already have it.

If you not get the others, do not get frustrated and continue in the effort, perhaps with time you can get them.

In relation to your friend Peter, he knows that happiness is within ourselves and that's why he don't seek out. He knows he has the basic needs and that is why he is happy, if he left some money for leisure it is good and if it is not, nothing bad happens.

Your friend Peter has a positive, proactive attitude and is grateful. These attitudes along the savings are essential to live in peace with ourselves and have a pleasant life.

Your problem to achieve happiness is where you focus your attention. You put it in what you don't have and he put it in what he has. You do not have to be perfect to bring a richer and happier life. Just be thankful for what you have. Do not give it all for granted.

Don't you think that you can always keep what you have, you can lose it at any time. Be grateful when you're at home, that just turning the switch on you have light, you turn the key and water comes out.

The day you wake and there's no light, or there's a water cut and you stay hours without running water. It bothers you, right? Well, appreciated when you have them. Keep in mind that nothing is eternal, so while you have them, enjoy them.

Regard to success, you misinterpret that. Success does not make you happy, it is quiet opposite. Being happy makes you successful. Because you appreciate what you have and what it take you to get it, the feelings that you sensed when you did it.

> **Do not let the things that you want, make you forget what you already have.**

Judge yourself for what you are able to create and not by your possessions:

What you have today, you may no longer have it tomorrow, however, which you are able to create will always be with you. Spends more money on experiences than acquiring material objects.

The more experience you have, the more issues you could discuss with yours. People will feel comfortable around you and remember you for what you are and not for what you have.

You will always carry your memories with you, anywhere you are, you will remember those special moments or those times when you felt so well and can relive those feelings. Nobody could never take that from you.

There are people who with their simple presence revitalizes any situation or place. You can get a smile just by the fact of being near them. Create a pleasant, friendly and relaxed atmosphere. Exude a contagious energy.

If you are a person who buys friends, I mean, that always pay... The beers at the bar, when you go to the movies, or at any time when money is in the middle, you assume the cost. If someday you need the money, you'll be alone. Your friends are used that you always pay, you are associate to a moneymaker. When the source is dry, there's no one interested.

However, if you are a person that gives off energy, they love you because the good atmosphere you create, you make people feel comfortable near to you. You pay occasionally, invest in social relations. When you meet your mechanic down the street and invites him a drink or to any other acquaintance, without being a close friend.

You are investing in social relations. When you have to search them for whatever reason, you will be attended better, they will be more involved. If one day you run out of money, your friends will not leave you behind. They are with you for the good you bring them. Not for your money.

> **Hang out with your loved ones at least once a week.**

The artists:

These people are remembered for their work, not their fortune. When you heard about one, immediately their work comes to your mind. That's what it is, to create. Create your life, do not buy it.

Earlier I mentioned the positive attitude and proactive attitudes, I will explain what they are.

People can be positive, proactive or reactive.

Reactive attitudes are more related to negative people and the other two attitudes are related to positive people.

Positive attitudes and proactive attitudes:

Positive Attitudes: Tendency to see and interpret what happens around us in a positive way or a favorable way. Faced to a conflict situation, tend to see the positive, always realistically. Understands them as challenges to face and overcome.

Dealing positively to emotional impulses and behavior and regulate them. Be aware of your own and others feelings. Show empathy and understand other´s points of view. Use positive social skills when interacting with others and most importantly, consider positive goals and make plans to achieve them. Always realistically, know that adverse situations have a positive side.

Proactive attitudes: Responsibility in front of one´s life, values precede feelings. They are as happy as they want, have self-regulation and responsibility to meet goals and objectives. They have full control of their behavior, they do it actively.

This implies taking initiative in the development of creative and bold actions to generate improvements. Making prevail freedom of choice on the circumstances of the context.

Proactivity means not only taking the lead, but, take responsibility for making things happen, always decide what we do and how we will do it.

Now that I'm talking of proactive people I will talk about reactive people.

Reactive people: They are the opposite of proactive. A reactive person has no plans. It is part of someone else 's plan. They believe that their situation does not depend of their actions and that only others can change their situation.

Postpones, not advance, stays where it is due to lack of goals and strategies. Justifies all the time and not take action, so leave things halfway, almost never finishes what starts.

Your friend Pedro is studying to be a lawyer, it is his motivation to keep working at the factory. Grateful to have a job, even if not earn a lot but it is enough to pay for his studies and debts owed to the bank. As he went to live with his parents, make it to the end of the month is no longer a problem.

Peter has adapted to the new situation and in bad, has found good and clings to it. He knows that is temporary and better times will come.

> **Negativity brings nothing new or good.**

An optimistic and proactive person, never asks:

Why? But, what for? events happen, whether positive or negative.

Knows that depend on the prism used to be seen. By simply changing this question the range of responses opens.

The *why?* makes you a victim and *what for?* opens the doors to new experiences.

To the questions of *why?* Always negative responses follow: I deserve it, I´m incompetent, I´m jinxed, that is who I´m, others are smarter than me, etc...

Instead, to the questions of *what for?* Always follow positive answers: Find the lesson contained in that frustration, in that loss, that pain, I must do better, I must focus more on what I do, learn other forms of behavior, offers the opportunity to improve in life.

> **The *why?* makes you a victim and *what for?* opens multiple answers.**

Rather think *I would prefer* than *I should*:

Concerning to our demands, we must change the mentality of *should* for *prefer*. It produces less frustration and control over our emotions and makes us more tolerant.

One of the keys to emotional health, is practicing tolerance to frustration. This is, accept that the world does not turn in the direction you want or things not always come out just the way you like. It is to accept that sometimes things are in our favor and sometimes not and we must tolerate these discomforts.

This is a reality that many people refuse to accept and feel really bad, and that is because their irrational beliefs about the world. They think in terms of *should*: "The world should be like I want," and when this is not fulfilled, become anxious or depressed.

The *should* requires that a particular situation should be as we want, without any changes.
- Everyone must treat me well, if not I get angry.
- Everything must be this way, if not, I do not like.

Instead, *prefer*, softens the situation. If is not as you want, you can always change and find one that suits best.

Thinking in *prefer,* would be:

- I'd prefer that you all treat me well and if not, there will be someone who treats me well.
- I prefer everything to be this way, and if not, I´ll look for the most appropriate.
- I prefer that the world was this way, if not, I will adapt to it.

Is not the situation or adversity that is directly causing your emotional distress:

No one and nothing has power over our emotions though we believe so, unless we permit it. When someone tells us something and we feel offended or a situation causes us discomfort.

What really happens is that we interpret that word or situation as bad and react accordingly. With our beliefs and thoughts, we give ourselves suffering.

A typical case would be: My boss crisp my nerves.
Mistake, your boss doesn't have the power to crisp your nerves.

What happens is that your boss says or does something and you, with your beliefs and thoughts look at the situation and feel like you can´t take it. In this way, the model semaphore clear all these concepts and you will see the relationship between thoughts and emotions.

Traffic Light Model:

- Red: Think, in relation to emotion.

- Yellow: Stop, there's an emotion.

- Green: Act, in consequence of the interpretation of the emotion.

YELLOW would be the trigger situation, adversity or problem, RED would be our thoughts and beliefs and GREEN are the consequences of those thoughts. That is, how we are emotionally and how we behave.

Summarizing:

You walk down the street and a situation with their emotions arises you. Caution you are in YELLOW.

Stop and analyze the situation, what happened? is it bad or good? how can it affect you? You are in RED.

Act, do you run away? or quite the opposite, it is not a big deal and you continue your walk. You are GREEN. We are free to decide how to act.

If someone is insulting you in a language you don't know, you'll not take it. You are ignoring the words.
The words are RED in the previous model. You'll be GREEN and will continue your way undisturbed.

But when we use the *irrational* label, that are not based on a logical or aren't realistic, are thoughts that go through our heads automatically without a reasoning process that question or confront reality.

As a result of this thoughts, people suffer exaggeratedly and do not act in the best way.

The problem with these beliefs is that, as its name suggests, the person believes them completely and does not sees other proposals or alternatives.

> **The others can´t decide our emotional state. They influence it but notdecide it.**

Invent your life, participates in it, direct it to where you want. Do not be afraid to go wrong, what is going to happen, that you learn a lesson? Perfect, you'll have something more to tell.

Continuing with your friend Peter, although his work not pleases too much, he knows that life is short and fleeting.

Spends a third of it sleeping to enjoy the other two, but one of these he spends working. That is, it is only one-third left for leisure and enjoyment. If you manage to do from work, a leisure, you will have two-thirds to enjoy.

If you have a job you do not like but you can´t quit, apply these three steps to yourself:

The three steps to appreciate your job:

1. Remind yourself why you have that job and what the rewards are: Make a list of what you like and what you don´t like. The important thing is to value the job you have and the effort you had to do to get there. This question will change your attitude towards work. With these reflections, you 'll appreciate it more and you will adapt better.

2. Turn your work and your space into something enjoyable: Find a way to be in a position to enjoy what you do. Create a comfortable and pleasant space, make the workplace your home. Adapt it to your circumstances and not the opposite.

If you are able to turn it into a hobby, you will never dislike going to work because you might associate with something fun.

3. Find the value of your work, have initiative: Value your work, give the value that it deserves. It is very important to give recognition and be proud of it, is an important tool in order to begin to love it. Work dignifies the person, gives added value to society. It will make you feel useful.

Another plus to not suffer at work: When you want a partner do something for you, instead of demanding, suggests. It is less aggressive and less bossed. In addition, you give a margin of decision and that produces personal satisfaction.

I mentioned that nothing is eternal, that any time you can lose it, well, that applies to your income too.

The importance of saving:

It is essential to keep these needs cover for the rest of your life without any problem and when no longer able to work or earn money, you can have an income that will allow you to maintain your desired life´s level.

I know you'll say: I already have the retirement pay. Let me tell you something: That's true, but with the amount that you will get, you won´t reach or maintain your standard of living. It will be just enough to cover the basic needs. You cannot allow any whim.

You'll go from work and having an income that allow you to have the desired life to be retired with a minimum income that is going to condition a limited lifestyle.

> **If you have not saved during your working stage, you will not be able to enjoy your retirement stage.**

According to statistical studies on the average life, this is 81 years. This means you have to live about 16 years more, once you stop having an income from your salary.

As for life quality that we can enjoy during our retirement it is closely related to the health that we have at that time.

Nutrition and physical activity are the keys to know how we age and live during our existence. A healthy diet and relatively

intense physical activity are the foundation to live better and have a healthy body.
We are what we eat and the best is a balanced diet for many years to maintain a good level of flexibility.

With these simple habits, you can reach old age in a good shape:

- Exercise daily, from 45 minutes to one hour.
- Sleep enough, depending on each will be 6 to 8 hours.
- Don't stress a lot, nothing is so important. If not depends on you, it makes no sense to worry, you can't do anything about it. And if it depends on you, you'll find the solution.

Sports are healthy in two aspects:
First, it keeps us in shape physically, and second, we relax mentally.

When you finish a training session, you end tired and just want to rest and relax. The problems you might have no longer seem so important.

Besides, those you couldn't find the solution, now as magic, it comes to your mind different alternatives and ways to solve them.

> **We will always carry our body with us and if we don't want to be a burden, let's take care of it.**

Save always 20% of your incomes:

Let's see, you earn a salary of 2.000 euros per month.
Imagine that you have always earned that amount and have saved 20% each month. It's 400 euros and 4.800 euros per year. Say you hire a deposit, 2% per year, that's a profit of 96 euros. Add those 96 to 4.800, it's already 4.896 euros in one year.

You start saving at 20 years old. Saving this amount for 45 years, it's 4.896 x 45 = 220.320 euros. But actually, it's more, because we have calculated the 2% 4 of 4.800. But when you had 20.000 euros, were 400 euros and not 96 and so on.

As you had more money, you had more because the interest. But don't add it to make up the difference that you'd had from your salary during these 45 years. Because now you earn 2.000 euros, but maybe 10 years ago, you earned 1.500 euros.
Following the lesson, now with 220.320 euros you can negotiate another interest because the more money you have, better products and benefits the bank offers. Let's say 5% annually, it would be a benefit of 220320 x 5% = 11.016 euros. Divided by 12 months comes to 918 euros per month.

That is, you will have a retirement payment equivalent to slightly less than half of your current salary. You can also choose to buy an apartment and not having to pay rent. Either way, you have the option to choose the lifestyle for your retirement.

It will be only matter of do the maths and decide the best option for you. In this case is only 20%, imagine 30%...

Now you tell me that is a very high percentage and it is impossible to save. You'll also ask: Why 20% and not 10% as most economists recommend?

I will start by answering your second question: The answer is easy, because 10% is very simple to save. However, from 20% you have to sit and think, where the money is spent and how to live the month with the rest of the income.

This amount of savings invites to question how to acquire more income and investment.

Regarding the first question:

What if your father, because life circumstances, low your salary by 20%? You will adapt, right?

You'll also tell me that your friends do not save and everyone thinks that doing so is a waste of time, the bank will keep all your savings, because it is not reliable.

Ask them how much money they have and will surely respond they have nothing. These people blame the world, society, the crisis, their boss, their misfortunes.

They do nothing to improve their situation and if someone wants to progress in their environment, they put stones on their way, discouraging with baseless arguments.

They are envious and surround themselves with people like themselves, thus, reinforce their attitude.
They don't want to leave their comfort zone, and conform do not risk for fear of failure. Choose not to be responsible for what happens in their life.

They fear failure because instead of seeing it as an opportunity to learn from their mistakes, see it as a reflection of their incompatibility.

Neither they want to bother to acquire financial intelligence retirement leave for tomorrow in state/government hands.

Moreover, they not realize that if with their current salary they struggle to make it to end´s months, with the retirement, which will be lower, they will struggle even more.

Saving for retirement is as important as fuel for the car.

Regarding to financial intelligence, now I´ll explain what it is.

Financial intelligence:

Is the kind of skill and knowledge that allows people to learn how to generate resources to live as they wish. The ability to solve or avoid financial problems. It helps to understand the productive world, how to apply their personal skills and exploit them to produce profits.

It's to search economic independence but not depend on a fixed income. Acquire assets that generate passive income to pay their lifestyle.

Easy, now I'll explain the type of mindset that you must have to successfully bring this process without overwhelm: you may think it is a pay for the work well done, your reward by get up early every day to go to work and worrying about your financial future.

If you think about it, the truth is that you pay everyone first before yourself. Pay for housing, food, electricity, taxes and if there is anything, save.

But it must be the other way, pay yourself first, because the more you earn, the more you will spend. It is a true story.

Once you've saved that percentage, proceed to pay others, you'll seek ways to do it. The need to pay others encourage you to find ways to do it.

Moreover, the fact of paying that percentage will make you question if you win enough to have that desired lifestyle. It will motivate you to ask yourself other ways to earn more, as they can be, asking for a salary increase, work more hours, changing for a better paid job, make investments or professionally studies.

By following this method of savings, you can enjoy life even more, its pleasures...You'll have the remainder money to spend or invest in order to have more, it's a personal choice.

Later I'll talk about investment.

You will not feel guilty about spending and you feel good about reward you with what you like and the effort made to achieve your goals.

> The more you earn, the more you will have to enjoy.

To make this process successfully, ask yourself:

How will be your financial future?
Where do you want to be in a few years and how?
I mean, where do you spend your money, if you make investments or not, and if you do, in what you invest? Think of 5 people with whom you relate and you'll be the average of them.

The human being behaves according to their peers.

Learn by imitation, acquires customs, habits and ways of thinking similar to those of their environment. Of the issues that you talk to them, it is what you will do. If you talk about investment, you'll invest, if you talk about how hard it is to make money, it will be difficult to earn.

To be fine in the economic sphere, you must be surrounded by both rich and poor people.
From the rich you will learn what to do to get where they are and from the poor, what not to do.

Like I said before, ask yourself:

What for? this will give you the answer to the *how*.

The three habits to always have money:

- Do not spend more than you earn.
- Always Save 20% of your incomes.
- Invest a part of the remaining money once you keep the savings.

The banks:

I'll say a few things about banks: They are not your enemies. Moreover, if you know how to work with them, they can be a good ally for your finances.

They can lend you the money you need.

The bank is a private company that lives from leave and retrieve money with interest added, plain and simple.

If you could not pay through the bank, electricity, rent, telephone and any other monthly or yearly expenses such as taxes, you would have to physically go to all these places to pay them in person.

With the inconveniences that it represents, you would have to stop working to go, thus, you lose hours of work. They leave us credit cards to buy whatever we want without having to carry cash.

You can travel around the world without carrying cash with you. If you need it, you go to a cashier and you take out money. It is normal to be charged a commission, they are providing you a service... you don´t pay for the waiter service?

If we want, we can pay monthly, with interest added. It becomes an instant loan. In addition, many credit cards charge the amount the following month, on day 5 or so.

This means that if your payday is day 1 of each month, you can make any purchase on day 2 and until the following month you´ll not to be billed.
You've been paid twice before actually paying the purchase. It's like finance two installments without any interest.

I´ll explain with an example to better understand:

Say James, always get paid the 1st of each month, he wants a TV that costs 600 euros. Today is payday and decides to go tomorrow to buy it, he spent 600 euros.

Until the next month he would not be billed and as he will be payed again, this will not suppose an economic effort. It is as if he would have paid in 2 times. 300 euros each time.

Do not misunderstand, I'm not defending banks.

I just want you to understand the importance of acquiring and investing in financial intelligence. You should go to the bank at least once a week, just to say hello to employees.

If you go to your friend's house to visit, why you will not visit those who take care of your money?

As they say, friction makes the love it will come a time where you come along well, which, when you want to invest, you may advise better. They´ll give you more attention.
If you only go to the bank in payday to get your money, for them will be just another number, as they do not know you.

The bank allows this way of buying, so they are not that bad.

> **If you hate banks, you´ll never get anything out of them.**

I summarize some advantages of credit cards:

- To solve some emergencies, such as unexpected travel, hospitalizations, emergency vehicle repair, appliances, etc.
- Pay services automatically by phone or Internet.
- Provision of cash any day of the year at any time through ATMs. All vantages.

You just have to be aware of their use. If paid monthly installments there is an interest that is added to the total amount, don´t think that is money given away.

> **The bank is not an NGO.**

Now I'll show you three ways to spend money and how to enjoy it.

Find out on what and how money is spent:

1- Live at day (*hand to mouth*):
These people spend everything they earn, the more they earn, the more they spend. As they know they will receive an extra income, they know already in what they're going to spend it. They do not think about tomorrow, for them there is only the present. They live in fear of death, their thinking is: What if I die tomorrow?

Consequences: They live carefree, drifting like a leaf in the wind, falling from a tree. From one side to another, without direction, without desire of self-improvement, they have no financial worries. Their greatest joy is payday. They are paying fixed payments.

They have calculated by millimeter, housing, groceries, whims, etc. They have not even one euro at the end of the month. The problem arises when they have an unexpected expense as it may be, car repair, the refrigerator, the lack of clothing, etc. If all these unforeseen arrive at once, they must choose which one they can pay.

If they planned to go on vacation they are no longer able to leave. That's when they put their hands on the head for not being able to cope with these expenses.

They are literally bankrupt.

That month they have to stop paying housing, electricity, telephone or any other fixed expenses and start being defaulter, pay the unexpected whatsoever. Because the amount of money they have is the same.

2- Living beyond their means… on credit:
These people spend more than they earn, they live on credit, pay everything with a credit card or loan and pay monthly. Mortgaging their future buying things they do not need with money they do not have, to impress people who are indifferent to them.

They want all at once, the house, furniture, car, travel, eating out, holidays, etc. These people do not give value to time, often think that nothing will change. That they will always keep the job, not get sick and that nothing bad can happen to them.

They tend to be impatient and impulsive, if they want something, they buy it. They do not accept their economic situation and want to live as if they were rich but ignoring that they buy things with incomes from their assets.
Rich people buy assets first.

Consequences: They live in luxury, are not deprived of anything, are capricious, they want everything at the moment. They are anxious, because as they want everything at once and not have the money, they have to borrow and waiting for the answer keeps them guessing.

The problem comes when the monthly payments of their loans begin to exceed their income or the financial institution no longer finances them more. Now the headaches begin. Now how they manage to pay off their debts?

All they have purchased has no longer the same value when acquired, even if they sell everything, it will be not enough to pay their debts.

But another problem is if their earnings are reduced, such as a salary decrease or dismissal. Now they have a serious problem, the bank is going to stay with all its assets and they will poorly until they pay their debts.

3 -Live saving a portion of the incomes:
These people live below their possibilities but without depriving their self, they are stark. When they want something, they have the money to buy it because they have previously saved. They are usually patients and reflective people.
Before buying, they ask if they have the money to buy such an object and if they do not, they save and then buy it. They know they can have it all, but not at the same time. Each thing at it's time. The house, furniture, car, holidays and others.

Consequences:
They live comfortably, carefree, like people who live by day but with the difference that if an unforeseen arises, they will be able to face it.

They can choose their way of life, they can do as if there were no tomorrow, making the most now, have dinner at the best restaurant in town or enjoy a romantic weekend.

They are farsighted, and have enough money to face it as they are savers, when they go walking around town they will see offers that may be.

They postpone immediate pleasure to achieve the target over the long term.

Save gives them security to buy anything, as they know how far they can go and negotiate the final price, because with the money in the hands you can get better prices. Is not the same to pay in installments that immediately, the second way, good discounts and better deals are available.

> **The three forms are equally valid. Choose the one that best suits you.**

I will capture these three ways of living in the cases of Lucy, Jane and Noelia:

The three friends go shopping and passing by through a travel agency they see an offer, a stay in the Maldives. Hiring it today, it has a 50% discount.

Noelia, the first thing that goes through her head is, come on, let's go and get the trip.

Jane, meanwhile thinks, the credit card is at its limit, I will have to ask them to let me finance it. But then, it will be no longer an offer as it will have to pay interest.

For its part Lucy knows she can´t afford it, she doesn't have enough money. She can´t go on a trip with her friends.

Can you imagine everyone´s lifestyle?

In fact: Lucy lives a day, *from hand to mouth*, Jane lives beyond her means and Noelia is thrifty.

Jane might think: I will do as Noelia, I'll save a part of my income each month and with the interest generated I could travel next time. But as it is impulsive and impatient she prefers to finance the trip, going further into the debt wheel.

She says to herself:

If Noelia can afford it, I also can do it but she don´t stop to think that her friend has been previously saved.

The interest she will pay to the financial institution, Noelia have been paid it to herself.

Lucy, however as no money, so she doesn't even think about it. In her way of life there is no room for the unexpected. Either good or bad, she just does not think about the trip.

She doesn't know how to manage money, she is unable to think of more expenses that the basic of the month.

As the days go by, if there is something left she is already looking how to spend it. But she does not get into debt, she does not have money but she doesn't owe to anyone. She doesn't even think about asking borrow.

Paying yourself, it's just financing yourself. Just at the inverse order, first save for the product and then you can enjoy it. With the interest you don´t pay you can have a better product. Is the case of Noelia.

Do not be ashamed of your economy:

If you are ashamed of your financial situation and you care about what others may think about you, I suggest you to try this:

Charles has an old car that spend more time in the mechanical workshop than circulating on the streets, Charles want to buy a new one but its economy will not allow it. He feels bad because all his friends have new cars.

He thinks they underestimate him because his car and he can´t take it anymore. Has the idea that a new car will help him to be seen in a better position.

His wife tells him: Since you want a new car but we only can afford to repair our old Ibiza, and I know this situation bothers you because all your friends have their new cars, let me give you a solution:

Let's go to the bar where you meet every day with them and when it is full, let me speak and don´t say a word.

When was the time, she yells to her husband:

- Charles, we are not going to buy the Golf!
- Do not you see that all your friends have lower class cars.
- What do you want? do you want to be presumptuous? You can not boast of anything else than a car?
- Repair the Ibiza and give a job to the poor mechanical.
- You know very well that I want the Porsche and not golf.
- You are selfish!

At the same time, she invites his friends to intervene and confirm what she is saying.

> **Do not feel inferior for having less possessions than others.**

Purchases:

Regarding to the purchases you do and they not satisfied you, the next time you go to buy something, ask yourself:

Why and what for do you want it?
What happens if you do not buy it?

If the answer is nothing, then do not buy it or just wait three months to see if the urge to buy it is still in your head, chances are it's no longer there.

Might be you want to buy it because the advertising or your friends influence.

We must tell the difference between our needs and the established by culture or the people around us.

Now that you know the reason of your concern and how to overcome it. I'll talk about the assets and liabilities mentioned above and the two mindsets about money.

Assets and liabilities:

An asset is any product that generate an income and a liability is otherwise, any product that generate expenses.

A passive income is any income that an asset generates.

In summary:

Assets: Buy real estate, properties to rent. Shares and investment funds that generate dividends and by selling them, we won more money than it cost us or at least we don't lose money.

Liabilities: Buy real estate and properties to live. Also any product which depreciate over time.

The case of real estate and properties is very peculiar, because if we live there, will give us an expense either monthly or yearly. In this case, they are passive. You have to pay taxes on them and some living expenses. Communities, and insurance reforms. They will be never ours. Interestingly, oddly enough, somehow we share it with the state.

If we do not pay taxes, they could seize the property. Instead, if we have them to rent, the income generated is already a profit with which to pay the cost of maintenance. In this case, they are active. This benefit is what is called a passive income.

As taxes increase, we increase the rent and the balance of the economy remains stable.

Buy assets has to become our favorite hobby.

Reached this point, surely you will ask me: Spending money to purchase pet is a passive, right?

My answer is no. It is not to spend in liability just like that, because this passive will generate welfare. Whereupon, you are investing in an asset, it will generate health. Is directly related to what I mentioned above about the basic needs, you are satisfying relationship with others. Love. Feel comfortable in your home and your loved ones in order to share moments of joy.

Later I'll talk about the form of financing to acquire assets and liabilities, debts. I will continue with the differences between the two mindsets about money.

Poor and rich mentality:

Poor mentality is based on relying solely on one source of income. The employee, its salary and the employer, of its business. They have no financial intelligence. It's a mindset focused on scarcity.
They just realize that terrible mistake if they lose that source. Anyone can have this mentality.

Does not distinguish between income, occupation, education, age or social status. They are not very cautious people, spend based on income, save only to spend.

Save to contingency, vacation, a car or any other passive and when they get it, they stop until they have another craving. They do not care about acquiring assets.

The thing about saving for incidentals, is that as already saving for them, always appears some.

No matter how small, they come for those savings. Their bank account just goes up from one year to another, in any case lows.

When they want to buy something and do not have enough money, they begin to reduce expenses in order to buy what they want. As they depend on a single source of income, as this decreases for any reason, have to stop spending on one place to spend elsewhere.

Instead, the rich mentality is totally different, people who think this way have financial intelligence. See business opportunities where poor mentality sees problems. They want to know their limits and therefore they are not afraid of failure, they know it is an opportunity to improve their learning.

This form of learning, in psychology we call it, *learning by Trial and Error.*

They are cautious and are always looking for other forms of income, besides what they already have, save their percentage of their incomes and in top of that they invest. They know the difference between saving and investing.

Having money and poor mind set and money disappears. Rich mind set without money and money is created and multiplied.

Saving and investing is not the same thing:

Saving is leave the money in an account and not think about it until retirement.

Invest, it is to allocate part of the remaining money, the separate percentage for retirement, in buying assets. As they know this difference, they acquire assets that will generate the desired life's quality. They are aware that everything that exists in this life changes continually. The human being, wealth, climate, pleasures, etc.

They do not want to be dependent on a single source of income, they are aware of the risk involved. That only source is something borrowed, you can have it today but perhaps not tomorrow. They acquire different multiple sources. Looking for financial freedom, they want to spend without relying on a monthly income. Stop working.

With the income they receive from the assets they bought whatever they want, reinvest a part of them and spend the rest. Invest time and money in their financial education, they do not stop learning. Not conceive professional development without personal development.

Poor mind set just wait retirement to... well, retire. Instead, rich mindset try to get extra income in order to live retirement without depending on retirement.

When they cannot buy something, instead of thinking: *I can't*, they think: *How can I get it?*

This leads them to acquire new habits of behavior, that way, they learn new methods and strategies.

You have to think rich. Even if you win 1000, 2000 or 5000 euros...

Once you have your 20% section for retirement, invest a part of the rest of your income to generate more money. The money must be your slave and work for you and the interest generated, are their children. They will also work for you.

You told me that someday you will direct your father's clinic, but if you know nothing about finances, sooner or later you'll broke. In college you will have learned a lot about medicine, but certainly nothing about how to invest your money to generate more money... and neither about taxes.

You have to understand what taxes are for. They are necessary for a country to offer its citizens good public services. Some are free and others will be at low cost. It is believed that if you earn more, the more you pay.

However, it is not always the case. You can also enjoy delicious discounts if you know how they work. If you do not want or do not look yourself, for now, able to master this issue, you can go to a manager or an accountant to advise you. It is not knowing everything, but know to who attend in every situation.

If you are interested in finance, you will come to an economist, if you want to buy a property, you will come to a builder.

You're not going to ask for advice on how to make bread to a mechanic or vice versa.

The football player:

Is dedicated to play football and earn money for it, does its best he can because he have talent and is fully dedicated to that. Do not waste time and energy on tax issues because he has someone devoted exclusively to that. Most players have other businesses other than play football, they know that the income generated is temporary.

The Passerby and the Explorer:

It comes to life as a transient or an explorer.
The passerby, is the person who goes through life without enjoy it. Do not question anything, does what society demands, someone else lead the way and decide for him. Everything is fine.

Instead, the explorer, embeds on it. Savor everything that life offers, continually questions its way of thinking and acts. Makes the trends that the passerby follows.

The time that I mentioned earlier about debts has come.

Good debt and bad debt:

You'll have to invest in the business if you do not want to be obsolete regarding to medical equipment. If you are able to make good investments and generate more incomes besides of those that you already receive for treating patients, you'll have a good economic background.

But if the day comes to investing and the fund still has not filled enough to cover expenses, you have to get in to debt and there is when financial intelligence does its part.

Many people hate debts, even more, they panic because of debts. They do not know the difference between good debt and bad debt.

Debt as a form of financing is neutral.
Not bad, not good.

It is the reason for the debt that determines whether it is one or the other.

If you know what is a bad debt you'll avoid it at all costs and will use it only when is essential. But if you know to distinguish good debt you can use it in your favor to create business with other people's money.

Bad debt is the one that is acquired for personal use, such as a car, a trip or any object that loses value over time. Decreases the value of your capital and it does not represent any investment. In simpler words, it is the debt that you pay, which you have to pay with your own money. Mortgage your future.

Instead, good debt is one that increases the value of your capital because it is an investment in something that will be recovered over time. In simpler words, it is the debt that you do not pay, it´s pay by itself.

Borrow money and create a business, with the money you get selling the products you´ll pay the loan installments. It is the one that will allow you invest in the clinic, in consequence you´ll have more patients and therefore more incomes and those incomes will pay for the debts.

Know to distinguish between good debt and bad debt makes the difference between people who know how to handle money and those who don't.

Hence the importance of saving. When you go to borrow from the bank, depending on the amount of money you have and the way you manage yourself economically, it will influence the decision to grant it or not. The more money you have, the easier it will be and in top of that, you´ll have better repayment terms and interest. It is not the same having a bank account with 50,000 euros than on with 120 euros.

Saving is always beneficious and if you know how to invest, you´ll reach a certain financial freedom before retirement.

In this topic comes into play personal risk aversion. But this book it´s not about to become a millionaire, but you having savings. Whereupon, I will not delve into it.

How to pay several debts at once:

If you get multiple debts, start paying the small ones, regardless of the type of interest the others may have. This approach will give you confidence, when you see that you are liquidating debts.

If you start by the bigger debts, as time goes on and you don't see results you may be demotivated, lose interest and get frustrated.

Second part

So far, I have focused my interest writing about the importance of saving. In this second part, I focus on happiness.

Happiness:

When people are asked about what they want badly in life, most answer *to be happy*. But they do not specify.
So, what is happiness?

It is a subjective and relative concept, a mood that give us satisfaction.

Who is happy feels comfortable, glad and pleased.
Best thing about happiness is that you determine to be happy in every situation and at every moment of your life, because if your happiness depends on someone, that's you.

But even if you determine your happiness is not a decision, it is a fact. Everyone is happy, except that many people don't know.

As they begin to relativize and appreciate what is really important, they realize that they are happy. They have what it takes to be happy. There is so many things to enjoy and our time on earth is so short that suffering is a waste of time.

It is like John´s case, now that he relatives, is happy. He doesn't have more things than before or a different job, has simply realized the place where he has to focus.

Happiness is built not pursued, which requires a minimum of effort.

Occasionally you have to wonder:

What is expected from life?

According to the answer to this question, we will be passersby or explores, as I have explained above.

To have a satisfying life, the pursuit of pleasure does not contribute. However, the search for commitment and sense do it, being the most important the second one.

Pleasure matter if you already have both commitment and sense, then it is the icing on the cake.

Pleasure is momentary, is tasted when a goal is achieved, but if you don't have a sense for it, soon will be worthless.

Commitment is important because it pushes motivation toward the task, is the energy that keeps us going. It reacts as planned and successful to get a project move forward.

Sense is the most important because it is the meaning of life.

Looking for a meaning is the base to get up every morning and go ahead no matter what the circumstances. For life to have meaning has to be lived according to personal values, passions and abilities.

Do not let anyone or anything remove the smile on your face. While you smile you're not worried. It is a very interesting part of the emotions, they can never be two opposite at the same time.

Do what you want but assume the consequences of your actions. Remember that we live in society, thus, your freedom ends where others begin.

To be happy and fine with others, we must accept unconditionally both ourselves and others. It is accepting the other either way: Handsome or ugly, white or black, smart or not, having money or not.

Everyone can give us beautiful things, regardless of their external characteristics, as I said, are not important. In addition, to be free and not agonize, it is very important to accept people of our circle with its flaws and virtues, and not try to change them. The key is to accept and appreciate the virtues they have, because everyone has.

It is better to try to adapt us and understand them, because we may know the person but not its past or the circumstances that made them be like that.

> **Happiness is natural and simple, don´t complicate yourself pursuing it.**

Smile:

Constantly smiling releases endorphins that are good for your body. It releases accumulated stress, gives shine to your face, makes you look more attractive and feel happier. Lower your blood pressure and strengthens your immune system, it can open many doors in any field.

Moreover, if you speak with a smile your voice becomes sweeter, even when you do it through the phone. People will come closer to you, seeing your character reflected in the joy and zest for life. If for any reason, you feel sad or frustrated and want to change that mood, practice this exercise:

Smile in front of the mirror:

At first it will not come naturally but eventually you will get a genuine smile. Many times, the physical is transmitted to the mental, so if you try to smile, after a few minutes you'll feel better.

Learning:

Relative to learning, no one is indifferent to the words.
Be careful what you read, see and hear, because one ends up living what we read, see and hear.

The words are interpreted according to the mood and insecurities we may have at the time. Our thinking determines how we act and interpret our past, present and future.

Our past may haunt us or make us proud, depends on how we think about it. We can live the present with joy or misfortune and the future, we may believe that it will be wonderful or catastrophic. Each of our thoughts and words determines our future, you become what you think it is inevitable.

Many people live lamenting its past, wrong decisions, failure relationships or unfulfilled goals. Consequently, they condition their present and possible future.

The present is now, learn new forms of behavior and strategies to face past. With these new behaviors, we can perceive differently and understand that maybe it was the best thing that ever happened to us. Changing the way we interpret our past, we change the present and consequently the future.

Assume responsibilities:

Life is created step by step, we are totally responsible for our life. Do not give others the power to lead your life. Any situation where you are, you built it, not others. Do not be lazy and blame others for your misfortunes, because by that rule, you should also attribute your accomplishments.

Do not be like the fans of a football team, that when the team loses, they say: *The team has played awful and they suck.* Otherwise when the team wins, they say: *We won and we are so good!*

Always think positive and in abundance in front of any negative circumstances. The abundance you will give you a brainstorm and you will choose the idea that best suits the situation. Face it as a lesson to learn. It happened for some reason, now you do not know it and it's terrible but it can emerge something really wonderful. Be aware.

A single negative thought can ruin your day, as you detect one, change it for a positive one.

We have to remember all the good thing that happened to us during the day and use regularly affirmative sentences about our life: I like my job, I do what I want, I have good friends, I love my couple, etc. Also reward us with something we like for a job well done, whether eating chocolate, ice cream, movies, etc.

If you still trying to change that negative and turning it into a positive one you cannot, give up for a moment and leave it for later.

Take a moment each day to worry about the problems, let's say an hour and a half. This way, when a problem comes to your head you'll think: I leave it for its time.

When you think about a problem, write it down, that way you can give it latter all your attention. It can be anywhere but always at the same time, you'll end up making it a habit.

Using affirmative sentences makes us to focus more on them and make them bigger. We focus on them, so they become our top priority. Best thing about affirmative sentences are the emotions that accompany them, the joy in knowing that you have the life you want and that triggers other emotions such as excitement, satisfaction... the energy to continue that lifestyle.

It keeps you active, willing to always do something because you become grateful and savor taste what you have.

Many people believe that we come to life just to suffer, but is because they don't know about what I mentioned concerning to irrational ideas.

People who think this way is because no one has taught them another way of seeing life. They are reactive and they only know how to respond, they are waiting for something to happen to answer.

Learning at school:

If at school they taught that to be happy and live in society do not need to compete and be the best, everything would be different. If from small instead of rewarding us with notes to see who is the best, do so with Suitable and not suitable, we would not be as competitive among us. We know whether we were right or not.

To win does not have to be: If you lose, I win. They could teach us that in order to win, we can both be winners. If I win, you win and vice versa. This way of thinking enhance solidarity and sharing.

In school duties they could encourage teamwork. If we win all, each of us wins and vice versa. If you or I win, the team wins.
The school prepares us to be good employees and always be the best. We are treated as employees of the factory, begins and ends at a certain time and during the day we have some breaks, lunch, meals and snacks. If you arrive late unjustifiably they penalize us.

When we reach adulthood, we are already educated to be a good worker and start working lives to enter the system consumption of each culture.

This is Andrew and Luis case: Two friends and schoolfellows, they studied law. Andrew has outstanding grades in almost all subjects, Luis, has always approve by the minimum.

Once finished school, the two starts working at the same law firm.

Andrew, of ten cases he has led, won just one, and Luis from ten which has also led, won them all. This reflects that not everything is about the grades. At school, they just prepare us to be obedient and above all, make no mistake, because we are suspended for doing so. In real life, outside the classroom, mistakes are synonymous of trying other ways of doing things.

It is Luis methodology, besides from using the tools he learned in college, use others, also effective.
Such as empathy, cleverness, wit, playfulness and spontaneity. All these qualities are not enhanced in school, thus are inhibited. When a student tries to do things differently even if they are equally valid, it is suspended. Being witty or clever is not rewarded. Instead, being mechanical is rewarded, the exact repetition of what is learned.

Don't get attached to material:

Another factor to consider, is not getting attached to material. While you have it, enjoy it to the fullest but if you lose it, that should not affect you.

Material is just to enjoy it, not for our well-being depends on it. Before buying it, you were happy, if you lose it now, you must return to the previous state of happiness. If not, do not acquire it, its loss will cause you more discomfort than before when you didn't have it. Material is made for our enjoyment and not for us to be dependent.

| Material is to make us freedom, not enslave us. |

Fear of Death:

Another interesting factor that many people live with disgust, is the fear of death. There is no reason to fear death, in any case, be afraid of not live. We all know that we will die. We do not know how or when.

But we live in a society that makes us believe that we are immortal, that we'll live forever. We buy mortgages of 40 years, creams and products to rejuvenate, aging is not accepted. Nobody wants to grow old.
This pace of life makes people go against the current, with wear and attendant consequences for health.

No one prepares us for death, not at school or in the media, who have so much power to influence.

There is no debate about it. It is a taboo subject, which people fears. We all know that we will die but nobody assumed.

If you are sick, two things can happen: That you die or that you recover.

If you die, you free yourself from the physiological needs of the body that are so annoying: Hunger, cold and sleep. And if you survive, you will be humbler, more grateful and therefore happier. Free of the tremendous burden of guilt, of what people may say, the envy and you'll live every moment as if it were the last. So, why be afraid? When you have a problem that distresses you, think: What if you died right now?

Nothing, nothing would happen. Your loved ones cry a while, but get used to your absence. Whereupon, it is demonstrated that nothing is so important.

Has the value and importance you want to give it, decides whether it is worth being so concerned about this problem or not. What brings you after? Is it worth the time invested on it?

> No one knows the reason of life. We are in this world without asking and leave without want. Now you are here, learn and enjoy the process, always smiling.

Oscar´s case:

A few days ago, I was talking to a friend, he told me that he was tired of the life he has. He didn't like his work and as a result was arguing with his wife. He adores his wife, but the stress that causes his situation makes that when he comes home discuss with her.

He don´t know what to do, he has to pay the mortgage and car loan, so he can´t leave. My response was to ask him:

What would you do if you were told you had one month to live? he replied: I would withdraw my savings from the bank and I would go to the Caribbean with my wife.

I said: Well, imagine this situation and acts as such, because you do not know the time you have left, not a month, a week or a day.

Here it is again the importance of saving, this man has enough money to go on vacation unexpected.
It is not the same to overcome his current situation by staying home than going on vacations to anywhere in the world. He will return with a clear and calm mind, ready to live his life.

If he had to stay at home, surely surpass the situation, but would take more time and suffering.

Living being yourself:

Life is like a straight line beginning at point A and ends at point B. All the we take it, but a few come before others.
The important thing about this line is how to get to point B, did you come to live according to your beliefs and motivations or conversely, did you come to live as other?

If you live according to your beliefs and motivations, you are living in fear of not living. You will take any time to do what you love and enjoy as if it were your last minute of life. However, if you live your life like others, you are living with fear of death. You will no longer do what you like to please them before they die and you feel bad about it. You are about to put their happiness before yours.

Achieve the goals:

For any goal you want to achieve, first visualize how you will feel when you get it, and then begin to take steps to achieve it.

Start by drawing a long - term path divided into smaller goals, short and medium term, that take you closer to the ultimate goal or you'll end up abandoning the project.

At first you may have really wanted but if you do not have a system to guide you to take the necessary steps to get it, as time goes by you will go demotivating.

To achieve the process, you need:

- Self-motivation: is the energy that comes from within.

- Commitment: is willing to pay the price to achieve our goals.

- Adaptation and flexibility: when unforeseen circumstances or things are not as we thought, you must have the ability to make the needed changes.

- Organization: Set an order in our behavior and establish the necessary priorities.

Set a deadline for the ultimate goal and intermediate dates to go objectively checking the progress and correct if necessary.

If we want to be experts in martial arts, we must first enroll us in a gym. Attend regularly and go from belt to belt until we are a black belt.

You cannot be an expert without going through all these phases. The objective will be achieved as short term goal are achieve, that motivation will get us to the end without giving up on the road.

I leave you a guide to orient you so you can achieve your goals.

The guide to reach it:

1. Is it realistic?

2. Why and what for you want it?

3. Write it down, that way it becomes a goal. Put a dateline, pressure will be good for you otherwise, you will procrastinate, leave it for later or tomorrow.

4. How can you get it? Create a brainstorm to choose. When you have the right one, use it.

5. Think about how it will affect your life. Possible obstacles that may appear, how to solve them. It will help determine the benefits and cons.

6. Turning it into a habit, must be like going to work. Habits are created after 21 continuous days repeating the ritual and after three months, it becomes routine.

- I finish what I start and what I said, I do.

- Visualize yourself, think and act like as if you've reached your goal already.

- Your thoughts mark the path of your life, if you think about it, you´ll act accordingly.

Now it comes the hardest: to keep you motivated.

How? With reinforcements, both negative and positive

Positive reinforcement: means adding something to your life. For example, you could indulge yourself with a dessert after reaching a goal.

Negative reinforcement: is when you take something away. If it's something you do not want, it can be a reward. For example, you could allow yourself to stop doing a task for a week as a reward for achieving a goal. The task is "eliminated" from your life that week.

Reinforcement is more effective than punishment to maintain your motivation. Depriving yourself of things or punishing yourself for failure can also work but in small doses.

If you ever fall and you do not want to continue, remember the reason why, why did you start? and how did you feel when you proposed?

Lourdes and Mary case: they are two friends who want access to college for people over 25 years.

They decide to enroll in the academy that will prepare them to pass the corresponding exams.

The course begins in September and ends in June, when the exams take place.

Classes are 3 times per week, with a duration of 2 hours each. Lourdes goes to all and not miss any. Instead, Mary, the first two months also comes regularly but from the third, begins to miss classes often. She makes any excuse, it's raining, is sick, she has no time, etc. Lourdes meanwhile, is aware of the effort she has to make to get the precious access to college and she is not distracted by anything. It is very aware and in June, she gets her diploma... and Mary, not even take the tests.

Lourdes visualized how she would feel once gained access to college and what she would do with it. She prepared a system to guide her to take the necessary steps to achieve this, which marked the short - term goals and specific dates to achieve them. It served as a compass for her journey.

How many times have you heard phrases like: This year I'm dieting, I'll look for a better job, I'll open my own business, I'll save more money.

All these purposes are born with the best intentions, but for 90% of people, is just that, purposes.

This is the reason why majority do not achieve their goals because they do not have a system to guide them to take the necessary steps to achieve them. They don´t visualize.

If women who want to lose weight imagine them self with the bikini on the beach and men, without the belly leaning over the bathing suit, it's likely to do the diet. They would have the image in mind and it would be their motivation to keep going and not give up trying. Do not have a methodology to achieve your goal is like traveling and trying to get to your destination without having a map, or precise indications.

Leisure:

What to do in our spare time?

The long-term leisure is very important for maintaining mental health. It is necessary to clear the mind and to rest from the stresses of everyday life. Is important because it provides a flow of energy. Besides of being a way to spend free time, it is a way to socialize, to create new friendships and being with family.

Summarizing:

It is a set of occupations to which the individual may voluntarily surrender completely after being released from their professional, family and social obligations. To relax, have fun and feel relaxed to perfect their selfless training, or to participate voluntarily in the social life of their community.

Two types of leisure, liabilities and assets are distinguished:

Recreation liability is one that gives nothing afterwards, such as watching television. It requires no effort from us, simply pass the idle hours.

Asset leisure is one in which we invest time and dedication to develop personally and where we can enhance our creativity. For example, study or sports.

Hence the importance of leisure. Knowing the regenerative effect it has on our body, one could say it has a direct and inverse relationship with stress.

At more leisure, less stress. This is why the creation of the holiday, to prevent stress and other pathologies. But even knowing this relationship, there is more and more people diagnosed with depression and anxiety. Due to the pace of life we so consumerist today, many people have gotten into loans to those who cannot cope and had to access a second job or overtime. As a result, they don't disconnect.

Have invested in basic needs, now people prefer to cover other needs before the really important. We live in a society of appearances, many prefer to go hungry or cold, but having objects that boast. But when basic needs are neglected, the body warning us that something is sick.

The price to pay for other needs rather than basic, is very high. A sick body cannot enjoy anything, so you may have many possessions, but if not enjoy it, possessions are useless.

Pretending:

Finally, I will talk about being what we are not. That is the meaning of appear. Manifest what is not or don't have.

Appearance is a mean to achieve a goal and especially limited in time, if purchased as a lifestyle, it becomes destructive. An unsustainable pace of life is acquired over time and with mental and economic consequences that this entails. Debts, jealousies and discomfort.

It is the case of the young lawyer: He wanted to work in the most prestigious legal firm in his city.

For the day of the interview he rented an Armani suit, a watch brand Rolex, some Italian shoes, a sports car and met with management. He wanted to impress with his outfit. He got the job and returned all the rented stuff. He has already achieved its goal, to be accepted at the buffet.

Now, he will invent any excuse to justify that no longer has the car and enough money to dress Armani and go to work with more modest outfits.

With all the stories told in the book, I want to underline the importance of saving a percentage of income. Having money can solve any unexpected events, such as the young lawyer. He had money to rent its appearance and with it has achieved the desired job.

This book does not invite to conformism, but to fight for your dreams. But remember, if you do not get it, nothing happens. The world will not end there, keep trying.

If you have food and shelter for the day, you can be happy. If a homeless is happy having food for the day and a box for warmth, imagine you who do groceries at the supermarket, you have access to health care and a house to shelter.

"It's not happier who has more, but who still having everything, does not depend on anything to be happy."

¡Dear reader,Relativizes!

Compilation of motivational phrases.

1. *Never underestimate your accomplishments.*

2. *A simple change in your life can disrupt your whole environment.*

3. *Luck depends from the point of view from where you interpreter it, can be good or bad.*

4. *Complain and not act creates bad atmosphere in the environment.*

5. *Every cause has a negative side and a positive, lets focus in the positive side.*

6. *To fully enjoy we must share.*

7. *Work enough to have the necessary.*

8. *Life is a gift, don't waste it.*

9. *Make from work a passion not a necessity.*

10. *Do not let the things that you want, make you forget what you already have.*

11. *Hang out with your loved ones at least once a week.*

12. *Negativity brings nothing new or good.*

13. *The why makes you a victim and the what for opens multiple positive responses.*

14. *Others can't decide our emotional state. They can influence but not decide.*

15. *If you have not saved during your working stage, you will not be able to enjoy your retirement stage.*

16. *We will always carry with our body and if we don't want it to be a burden, let's take care of it.*

17. *Saving for retirement is as important as the fuel for the car.*

18. *The more you earn, the more you will enjoy.*

19. *If you hate banks, you will never get anything out of them.*

20. *The bank is not an NGO.*

21. *The three forms are equally valid. Choose the one that best suits you.*

22. *Do not feel inferior for having less possessions than others.*

23. *Poor mindset and money disappears. Rich mindset without money and money is created and multiplied.*

24. *You have to think rich. Either if you win 1000, 2000 or 5000 euros ...*

25. *To distinguish between good debt and bad debt makes the difference between people who know how to handle money and those who doesn't.*

26. *Happiness is natural and simple, do not complicate yourself pursuing it.*

27. *The function of material is to give us freedom, not enslave us.*

28. *No one knows the reason of life. We are in this world without asking and leave without want. While you are here, learn and enjoy the process, always smiling.*

Author´snote: I leave you reverse psychology patterns of behavior, as its name suggests, is reverse psychology. Do just the opposite:

Reverse psychology

1. **Get bored:** think that life is boring, you will not improve your personal situation, it will never change.
2. **Practice ingratitude and rudeness:** do not be educated, why say thank you and have a socially correct behavior, if life just bring misfortunes?
3. **Live in anguish for money:** constantly think you're about to lose your work or your money and you do not have enough to survive.
4. **Turn into a negative person:** take your negativity as far as possible and do not settle for anything. Have negative thoughts and constantly express them, behave in front of others as a depressed, insecure person, who is always sick and not stop complaining.
5. **Complain about everything:** Complain endlessly and do nothing to change the situation, others will do it.
6. **Don't trust in others and blame them for your misfortunes:** suspicious about theintentions of people around you, whether friends or relatives. Label them as false, which act because they want something from you, who feel superior to you and want to deceive or simply envy you. If something goes wrong in your plans, is their fault, never yours.
7. **Glorifies the past:** any past was better and this is clearly a disappointment. When you were younger, everything was better, it was a time of glory and celebration.

www.ingramcontent.com/pod-product-compliance
Lightning Source LLC
Chambersburg PA
CBHW071728040426
42446CB00011B/2261